Mr Bates

vs

The Post Office

Two decades of hidden injustice: how a TV Drama
Changed history and shook up Britain – in just a
week

Larry L. Knapp

TABLE OF CONTENT

INTRODUCTION

Have you ever wondered about the incredible power of television? How can a single TV show shine a light on a hidden injustice, inspire millions, and even change the course of history? That's the remarkable story we're about to explore in the pages of this book.

Imagine a real-life scandal that affected hundreds of innocent people, pushing them to the brink of despair. For nearly two decades, post office branch managers across the UK found themselves wrongly accused of theft and false accounting. Lives were shattered, families torn apart, and all because of a faulty computer system called Horizon.

The shocking details of this injustice were known to some, but they remained hidden from the wider public for years, buried beneath layers of bureaucratic red tape and legal complexities. Until one day, a TV drama burst onto the scene and changed everything.

"Mr. Bates vs The Post Office," a gripping four-part series, aired on the first day of the new year in 2024. Little did anyone know that it would become a catalyst for action, a force that would galvanize the public, shift public opinion, and even prompt the British government to take unprecedented steps.

In the following pages, we'll dive deep into this captivating story. We'll explore how the drama unfolded on our screens, how it captured the hearts and minds of viewers, and how it sparked a groundswell of support for those who had suffered the most.

But this isn't just a tale about a TV show's impact; it's a testament to the enduring power of storytelling. It's about how narratives, when told with passion and authenticity, can bridge the gap between our screens and our hearts. It's a story of real people, real pain, and the very real change that can come when we pay attention to the stories that matter.

So, join us on this journey through the world of "Mr. Bates vs The Post Office" and beyond. Let's explore how television can be a powerful agent of change, how it can amplify voices that need to be heard, and how it can inspire action in a world where sometimes, it feels like no one is listening.

Chapter 1

The Post Office Horizon Scandal

Background of the Post Office Horizon Scandal

Imagine waking up one day to find your life turned upside down, accused of a crime you didn't commit, and thrust into a legal nightmare that would haunt you for years. This was the harsh reality for hundreds of post office branch managers across the United Kingdom caught up in the Post Office Horizon scandal.

The story begins in 1999 when the Post Office introduced a new centralized computer system known as "Horizon." It was meant to streamline operations, improve efficiency, and bring modernization to the postal service. However, what was supposed to be a leap forward quickly descended into a nightmare for many.

Horizon was riddled with software glitches and errors that resulted in serious financial discrepancies. Branch managers who had served their communities for years suddenly found themselves facing accusations of theft and false accounting. Money appeared to be vanishing from their branches, and they were held responsible for these apparent shortfalls.

What made matters worse was the relentless pursuit by the Post Office itself. They not only accused their own branch managers of financial wrongdoing but also pursued legal action against them, demanding repayment for the alleged losses. This relentless pursuit through the courts threw the lives of these branch managers into disarray.

Wrongful Accusations and the Human Toll

The heart-wrenching aspect of this scandal lies in the wrongful accusations and the devastating human toll it exacted. For those accused, it was not just a matter of financial loss; it was the loss of reputation, dignity, and, in some cases, even freedom.

These individuals, who were pillars of their communities, faced public humiliation, strained relationships, and the emotional trauma of being branded as criminals. They lost their livelihoods, homes, and, in some cases, their health. Some were driven to the brink of bankruptcy, while others were incarcerated, including a pregnant woman who found herself behind bars.

One of the most distressing aspects was the Post Office's refusal to acknowledge the faults in the Horizon system. When the accused insisted that the discrepancies were due to software errors, they were met with disbelief and hostility. Instead of addressing the issues, the Post Office doubled down on its accusations, forcing many to bear the weight of guilt for crimes they did not commit.

The toll on mental health was profound. Many of the wrongly accused experienced anxiety, depression, and, in some tragic instances, even contemplated or carried out suicide. Families were torn apart, and the scars of this ordeal continue to affect them to this day.

As we delve deeper into the Post Office Horizon scandal in this chapter, we'll uncover the stories of those who endured this injustice, shed light on the magnitude of the crisis, and explore the journey of these individuals as they fought for truth and justice. This is a chapter that reveals not only the systemic failures but also the indomitable spirit of those who refused to give up in the face of adversity.

Chapter 2

The Persistence of Injustice

The Victims' Fight for Justice

In the face of overwhelming adversity, the victims of the Post Office Horizon scandal demonstrated an unwavering determination to fight for justice. They refused to be silenced, and their collective resilience serves as a testament to the human spirit.

Imagine being wrongly accused of a crime, facing financial ruin, and watching your life unravel. It's a nightmare scenario that would break many, but not these individuals. Instead, they banded together, united by a shared sense of injustice and a desire to clear their names.

The victims, primarily post office branch managers and sub-postmasters, formed a close-knit community. They began to share their stories, exchange information, and offer each other support. It was a grassroots movement born out of necessity, driven by a common goal: to expose the truth behind the Horizon system's failures.

Their fight for justice was not limited to emotional support; it extended to legal action. Recognizing the need for a coordinated effort, they initiated legal battles against the Post Office. These legal challenges marked the beginning of a long and arduous journey through the British legal system.

Legal Battles and Setbacks

The road to justice was fraught with challenges and setbacks. The victims faced formidable opponents in the form of the Post Office, a powerful institution with deep pockets and a vested interest in defending its reputation. What followed was a series of legal battles that would test the resolve of even the most tenacious individuals.

The victims' legal journey was marked by complexity and frustration. They were met with resistance at every turn. The Post Office vehemently denied any fault in the Horizon system, insisting that the accused were responsible for the apparent financial discrepancies.

The legal battles unfolded over years, characterized by lengthy court proceedings, costly legal fees, and emotional strain. For many, it became a battle not only for justice but also for their very survival. Some victims were forced to remortgage their homes, deplete their savings, or rely on the support of friends and family to finance their legal defense.

Throughout this period, the victims encountered setbacks that would have disheartened most. Court decisions sometimes went against them, and the burden of proof weighed heavily on their shoulders. The legal system, which should have provided a path to justice, often felt like an insurmountable obstacle.

Despite the odds, the victims' resolve never wavered. They continued to fight with determination, buoyed by the belief that they were in the right. Their dedication to uncovering the truth and holding the Post Office accountable became a rallying cry for justice.

Chapter 3

Mr. Bates and His Crusade

Alan Bates and the Group of Sub-Postmasters

Every crusade needs a leader, and in the fight against the injustices of the Post Office Horizon scandal, Alan Bates emerged as the indomitable force driving change. His journey from being an accused sub-postmaster to a relentless advocate for justice is nothing short of remarkable.

Alan Bates was not a household name or a charismatic public figure. He was an ordinary man thrust into an extraordinary situation. Like many others, he had dedicated years of his life to serving his community as a post office branch manager. However, when the accusations of theft and false accounting began, he found himself at the center of a maelstrom of legal battles and personal turmoil.

What set Alan Bates apart was his refusal to accept the unjust fate that had befallen him and countless others. He possessed a quiet determination and an unwavering belief in the truth. Recognizing that he was not alone in his plight, he reached out to fellow sub-postmasters who had faced similar accusations.

Together, they formed a close-knit group united by a common cause. They shared their stories, exchanged information, and provided emotional support. It was a support network that would become the bedrock of their fight for justice.

Launching Legal Action Against the Post Office

With Alan Bates at the helm, the group of sub-postmasters embarked on a journey that would test their mettle and resilience. Their objective was clear: to hold the Post Office accountable for the injustices inflicted upon them.

Launching legal action against a formidable institution like the Post Office was no small feat. It required courage, determination, and an unwavering belief in the righteousness of their cause. They were up against an opponent with vast resources and a reputation to protect.

The legal battles were complex and protracted, spanning years of courtroom drama. The accused sub-postmasters faced a relentless adversary in the Post Office, which vehemently denied any wrongdoing on its part. The burden of proof lay heavily on the shoulders of those seeking justice.

However, Alan Bates and his fellow sub-postmasters refused to back down. They were driven by a deep-seated conviction that they were fighting not only for their own exoneration but also for the countless others who had suffered in silence. Their legal battle was a David-and-Goliath struggle, a clash between individuals seeking truth and an institution unwilling to admit fault.

As the legal proceedings unfolded, the accused sub-postmasters encountered numerous obstacles and setbacks. Court decisions did not always fall in their favor, and the emotional toll of the legal battles was immense. Yet, they pressed on, bolstered by their collective determination.

Alan Bates, in particular, emerged as a symbol of resilience and unwavering commitment. His leadership inspired those around him to persevere in the face of adversity. He was not a charismatic orator or a charismatic figure, but he possessed a quiet strength that resonated with his fellow fighters for justice.

The Power of Television Drama

Chapter 4

"Mr. Bates vs The Post Office" – A Game-Changer

Overview of the TV Drama

Television has a unique power to captivate audiences and bring hidden stories to the forefront of public consciousness. In the case of "Mr. Bates vs The Post Office," this power was harnessed to shed light on one of the most significant miscarriages of justice in the United Kingdom.

Airing on January 1, 2024, "Mr. Bates vs The Post Office" was not just another TV drama. It was a groundbreaking four-part series that would prove to be a catalyst for change. The drama unfolded the decades-long torment of those accused in the Post Office Horizon scandal, translating their stories into a gripping narrative that would capture the hearts and minds of millions.

The show's brilliance lay not only in its storytelling but also in its timing. For years, the victims of the scandal had struggled to make their voices heard through traditional channels, but now, the small screen provided a platform that would amplify their stories to a vast audience.

"Mr. Bates vs The Post Office" was meticulously crafted by writer Gwyneth Hughes, who understood the power of storytelling to bridge the gap between facts and emotions. The series was designed to reach deep into the hearts of viewers, compelling them to care about the real people behind the headlines.

The Emotional Resonance of the Series

One might expect that a drama centered on computer system errors and accounting discrepancies would struggle to engage a wide audience. However, "Mr. Bates vs The Post Office" defied expectations by tapping into the emotional core of the Post Office Horizon scandal.

It humanized the crisis by focusing on the personal stories of those affected. Viewers were introduced to characters like Alan Bates, played stoically by Toby Jones, who became the embodiment of resilience and determination. Bates, an ordinary man caught in an extraordinary situation, led a group of sub-postmasters in their fight for justice.

The emotional resonance of the series was palpable. It brought to life the pain, anguish, and suffering experienced by the wrongly accused. As viewers watched these characters endure financial ruin, public humiliation, and emotional turmoil, they couldn't help but empathize with their plight.

Monica Dolan and Julie Hesmondhalgh, among other talented actors, portrayed the devastating toll the scandal took on individuals and their families. The series depicted the accused as real people facing an unjust system that seemed insurmountable.

Gwyneth Hughes, the writer of the series, achieved a remarkable feat by creating a "direct visceral appeal." Her storytelling reached out across screens and grabbed viewers by the throat, compelling them to care deeply about the characters and their quest for justice.

The drama served as a powerful reminder that behind every legal battle and bureaucratic delay were real lives hanging in the balance. It showcased the resilience of ordinary individuals who refused to be silenced, even when the odds were stacked against them.

The emotional resonance of "Mr. Bates vs The Post Office" was not confined to the screen. It transcended into the real world, sparking a groundswell of public support and outrage. Viewers were not content to be passive observers; they wanted to see justice served.

Chapter 5

The Impact Unleashed

Public Reaction and Support

When the power of television storytelling converges with a compelling narrative, the result can be a profound impact on society. "Mr. Bates vs The Post Office" achieved just that by resonating deeply with the public, sparking a groundswell of reaction and support that would shape the course of the Post Office Horizon scandal.

As the series unfolded, viewers across the United Kingdom found themselves drawn into the harrowing stories of the wrongly accused post office branch managers and sub-postmasters. They witnessed the devastating toll the scandal had taken on individuals and their families – financial ruin, public humiliation, and emotional turmoil. It was a stark reminder that behind the bureaucratic complexities and legal battles were real lives hanging in the balance.

The emotional resonance of the series was palpable. It tapped into a universal human instinct – the desire for justice. Viewers were not content to be passive observers; they wanted to see wrongs righted and accountability established. Social media platforms buzzed with conversations, and individuals from all walks of life began sharing their thoughts and experiences related to the scandal.

The public's reaction was characterized by a mix of empathy, anger, and a desire for action. Stories of viewers reaching out to support the victims started emerging. People were moved to offer financial assistance, emotional support, and solidarity. The series had created a sense of collective responsibility to address the injustice that had persisted for far too long.

Paula Vennells and the Petition

One of the most visible manifestations of public outrage was directed at Paula Vennells, the former CEO of the Post Office. Lia Williams' portrayal of Vennells in the series was so convincing that it ignited a firestorm of public indignation.

Within days of the series finale on January 4, 2024, more than a million people had signed a petition demanding that Paula Vennells relinquish her CBE, an honor bestowed upon her by Queen Elizabeth II in 2019. Vennells, once a respected figure, found herself at the center of a public outcry.

The petition represented a resounding message from the public: accountability must prevail. The fact that so many individuals from diverse backgrounds were willing to add their voices to the cause showcased the power of collective action. It was a stark reminder that public opinion could not be ignored.

Government Response and the Promise of a New Law

As the groundswell of public support continued to grow, it reverberated within the corridors of power. The British government could no longer remain indifferent to the cries for justice that had been amplified by the series.

On January 10, 2024, Prime Minister Rishi Sunak made a significant announcement. He pledged to introduce a new law that would swiftly exonerate and compensate the victims of the Post Office Horizon scandal. This promise marked a sweeping intervention that aimed to finally bring justice after years of glacial progress.

The government's response was a testament to the impact of the series. It demonstrated that when a narrative resonates with the public, it can exert significant pressure on those in positions of authority. The Prime Minister's commitment to righting the wrongs of the past signaled a recognition of the deep-rooted injustices that had plagued the victims.

Television's Influence on Real-Life Issues

Chapter 6

The Historical Significance of TV Dramas

Previous Instances of TV Dramas Driving Change

Television has long been recognized as a powerful medium that can shape public opinion, challenge the status quo, and ignite social change. Throughout history, there have been several instances where TV dramas have played a pivotal role in driving real-world transformations. "Mr. Bates vs The Post Office" is the latest in a lineage of such impactful television narratives.

One of the most iconic examples of a TV drama catalyzing change is "Cathy Come Home," which aired in 1966. This British television play, directed by Ken Loach, centered on the struggles of a young homeless mother named Cathy. The gripping portrayal of her life and the systemic issues that led to her homelessness had a profound impact on viewers.

"Cathy Come Home" led to a national conversation about homelessness and housing policies. It drew attention to the plight of homeless individuals and families, challenging societal perceptions and prompting discussions in the House of Commons. The drama ultimately played a pivotal role in the formation of the homeless charity Shelter.

Similarly, the 2019 miniseries "When They See Us" by Ava DuVernay demonstrated the enduring power of TV dramas to effect change. The series fictionalized the real-life case of the Central Park Five, five Black and Latino teenagers wrongly convicted of rape in 1989. Although they were exonerated in 2002, the series brought renewed attention to the injustices they had suffered.

"When They See Us" not only highlighted the failures of the U.S. judicial system but also prompted discussions about racial discrimination and wrongful convictions. It resonated with viewers, reaching an audience of 23 million people in its first month of streaming. The series led to reparations for the Central Park Five and reignited conversations about racial justice in America.

Lessons from "Cathy Come Home" and "When They See Us"

Both "Cathy Come Home" and "When They See Us" offer valuable lessons about the historical significance of TV dramas and their potential to drive change.

First and foremost, these dramas humanized complex societal issues. They focused on the personal stories of individuals affected by larger systemic problems. By portraying the struggles, injustices, and resilience of the characters, the series connected with viewers on a deeply emotional level.

In "Cathy Come Home," viewers were compelled to empathize with Cathy's plight as a homeless mother, sparking conversations about homelessness and housing policies. In "When They See Us," the series shed light on the lives of the wrongfully accused Central Park Five, driving discussions about racial discrimination and the flaws in the justice system.

Additionally, both dramas harnessed the power of storytelling to bridge the gap between facts and emotions. They presented factual narratives in a compelling and relatable manner, making complex issues accessible to a broad audience. By doing so, they engaged viewers not only intellectually but also emotionally.

Furthermore, these dramas leveraged the influence of media to create a groundswell of public support and action. "Cathy Come Home" led to the establishment of Shelter, a prominent charity addressing homelessness. "When They See Us" contributed to reparations for the Central Park Five and renewed advocacy for racial justice.

The historical significance of these TV dramas lies in their ability to effect change beyond the confines of the screen. They sparked national conversations, influenced policy changes, and empowered individuals to take action.

Chapter 7

Addressing Social Issues through Television

"It's a Sin" and the AIDS Crisis

Television has the remarkable ability to address critical social issues and bring them into the collective consciousness. One of the most recent examples of this transformative power can be found in the British series "It's a Sin." Created by Russell T Davies, this drama takes viewers on a poignant journey through the heart-wrenching AIDS crisis of the 1980s.

The series revolves around a group of young friends in London who confront the emerging AIDS epidemic. Through their experiences, "It's a Sin" unflinchingly explores the devastating impact of the disease on the LGBTQ+ community and society at large. What sets this series apart is its raw emotional depth and its unwavering commitment to humanizing the characters affected by the crisis.

"It's a Sin " achieved a profound resonance with viewers, particularly younger audiences who had not lived through the AIDS epidemic. It served as both a history lesson and an emotional revelation, shedding light on the injustices faced by the LGBTQ+ community during that era. Lead actor Olly Alexander expressed, "Young gay people can't believe it happened," highlighting the series' role in educating a new generation about the struggles of their predecessors.

Moreover, "It's a Sin" had a tangible real-world impact. The Terrence Higgins Trust, a leading HIV charity, reported a significant increase in HIV testing following the series' release. This surge in testing represents a critical step toward ending new HIV cases by 2030, showing how television can drive proactive change in public health awareness and prevention.

"Pose" and Trans Representation

Representation matters, and television has the power to reshape societal perceptions and attitudes. The groundbreaking series "Pose" is a prime example of how television can address social issues, specifically trans representation and the LGBTQ+ experience.

Set in the vibrant ballroom culture of 1980s and early 1990s New York City, "Pose" not only features a predominantly transgender cast but also tells their stories with authenticity, empathy, and depth. The series delves into the challenges faced by trans and gender-nonconforming individuals, including discrimination, HIV/AIDS, and the struggle for acceptance and respect.

"Pose" has been hailed as "the most groundbreaking LGBTQ+ show ever" and has significantly contributed to reshaping the narrative around transgender experiences. The show's impact extended beyond the screen, with Michaela Jae Rodriguez, who played Blanca, becoming the first-ever trans actor to win a Golden Globe in 2022.

The series created a platform for transgender voices and stories, helping to humanize and destigmatize the experiences of transgender individuals. It has inspired important conversations about inclusion and representation in the entertainment industry and society as a whole.

"Dopesick" and the Opioid Crisis

The opioid crisis has been a devastating public health issue, particularly affecting working-class communities in the United States. The television series "Dopesick" brought this crisis to the forefront of public discourse, shedding light on the role of pharmaceutical companies, including Purdue Pharma (owned by the Sackler family), in fueling the epidemic.

"Dopesick" is a gripping drama that exposes the grim reality of opioid addiction and the corporate practices that enabled it. The series depicts the lives of individuals and families impacted by addiction, highlighting the pain, suffering, and loss caused by the crisis.

What sets "Dopesick" apart is its ability to humanize the victims and reveal the complicity of pharmaceutical giants in perpetuating the crisis. The series struck a chord with viewers who empathized with the struggles of those affected and felt outraged by the corporate greed that fueled the epidemic.

Following the broadcast of "Dopesick," there was a groundswell of activism and advocacy. Calls for major art institutions to reject funding from the

Sackler family, whose company profited from the opioid crisis, gained momentum. The Metropolitan Museum of Art in New York and numerous other institutions removed the Sackler name from galleries, demonstrating the tangible impact of the series on the art world.

The Future of TV and Social Change

Chapter 8

TV's Role in Shaping Public Perception

The potential for TV to raise awareness

Television has always been more than just a source of entertainment; it's a powerful medium that has the potential to shape public perception and raise awareness about critical issues. In Chapter 8, we'll delve into the profound impact that TV can have on the way we perceive and engage with the world around us.

Television has the unique ability to bring complex and often overlooked issues into the living rooms of millions of viewers. It's a medium that combines storytelling with visual and emotional elements, making it highly effective in capturing and holding the audience's attention. When used wisely, television can ignite conversations, inspire empathy, and drive meaningful change.

One of the key ways television raises awareness is by humanizing the stories behind important social issues. By focusing on the lives and experiences of individuals affected by these issues, TV shows can make distant problems feel immediate and relatable. Whether it's portraying the struggles of marginalized communities, the challenges of individuals facing discrimination, or the consequences of environmental crises, television can bridge the gap between facts and emotions.

Television also serves as an educational tool, providing viewers with insights into unfamiliar topics and encouraging them to question their preconceived notions. It has the power to challenge stereotypes, debunk myths, and offer a more nuanced understanding of complex issues. In doing so, television empowers viewers to become more informed and compassionate citizens.

The Impact on Policy and Public Discourse

The influence of television extends beyond individual awareness; it has the potential to shape public discourse and policy decisions. When TV dramas and documentaries tackle pressing social issues, they can trigger widespread conversations that lead to societal change.

A notable example is the way television has addressed issues related to racial discrimination and civil rights. Historical dramas like "Roots" (1977) and contemporary series like "Black-ish" have played a crucial role in advancing discussions about race, inequality, and representation. These shows have contributed to the broader dialogue on racial justice, influencing public perception and pushing for policy reforms.

Furthermore, television can serve as a catalyst for policy change. When a TV series sheds light on a systemic problem or injustice, it often leads to increased scrutiny and demands for accountability. This heightened awareness can mobilize advocacy groups, activists, and concerned citizens to push for legislative reforms and institutional changes.

A compelling example is the impact of the documentary series "Making a Murderer" (2015). The series examined the case of Steven Avery, who was wrongfully convicted of murder, and raised questions about the criminal justice system. It prompted public outrage and calls for criminal justice reform, leading to renewed efforts to address wrongful convictions and improve legal procedures.

Chapter 9

Stories that Matter

Upcoming TV projects addressing social issues

Television's role in addressing social issues is an ever-evolving and dynamic one. In Chapter 9, we'll take a closer look at upcoming TV projects that continue to tackle critical societal challenges and explore the evolving landscape of television's influence.

The power of television to shed light on important issues has not waned. In fact, it continues to be harnessed by creators and networks to tell stories that matter. These upcoming projects are poised to engage audiences in thought-provoking narratives and contribute to ongoing conversations about pressing social concerns.

One such project is the series currently in development about the 2017 Grenfell Tower fire in London, a tragedy that claimed 72 lives. The show aims to bring attention to the complex factors that led to the disaster, including issues related to housing, safety regulations, and inequality. By dramatizing the events and their aftermath, this series has the potential to ignite discussions about accountability, housing reform, and social justice.

Additionally, there are calls for television to explore the historical injustices related to the infected blood scandal of the 1970s and 1980s. This potential project could shed light on the lives affected by contaminated blood products and the decades-long fight for justice. By sharing these stories, television can play a vital role in seeking redress and acknowledging the harm caused to victims.

The diversity of upcoming TV projects addressing social issues reflects the medium's commitment to amplifying voices and stories that have been marginalized or overlooked. From racial inequality and LGBTQ+ rights to environmental challenges and healthcare disparities, television remains a platform for exploring the complexities of our world.

The Continuing Influence of TV in a Changing World

Television's influence on society is as relevant as ever, even in a rapidly changing media landscape. While streaming services, social media, and digital platforms have transformed how we consume content, television retains its unique capacity to reach a broad and diverse audience.

One enduring strength of television is its ability to create shared experiences. When millions of viewers tune in to watch a thought-provoking series or a compelling documentary, they become part of a collective conversation. These shared experiences can shape public opinion, inspire activism, and drive change.

Television also adapts to the times by embracing new formats and storytelling techniques. Limited series, anthologies, and docudramas have become effective vehicles for exploring social issues in depth. Creators leverage the episodic nature of television to delve into complex narratives and characters, allowing viewers to engage deeply with the subject matter over time.

Furthermore, the digital age has made television more accessible than ever. Streaming platforms enable viewers to engage with content on their own terms, making it easier for individuals to discover and engage with socially relevant programming. Online discussions, social media campaigns, and virtual watch parties have transformed the way we interact with television, fostering communities of viewers who share their perspectives and insights.

CONCLUSION

As we reach the conclusion of our journey through the power of television in addressing social issues, it's evident that this medium holds a unique and enduring place in our lives. It's more than just a source of entertainment; it's a storyteller, an educator, and a catalyst for change. In this concluding chapter, we'll reflect on the profound impact of television and its continued relevance in a rapidly evolving world.

Television has always had the remarkable ability to transcend mere screens and connect with the hearts and minds of its viewers. Throughout our exploration, we've witnessed how television has been a driving force behind awareness, empathy, and advocacy. It has served as a mirror to society, reflecting both its triumphs and its injustices. Through compelling storytelling and empathetic portrayals, television has humanized complex issues and brought them into our living rooms.

The journey began with an examination of the Post Office Horizon scandal, a stark reminder of how technological failures can have devastating human consequences. We delved into the wrongful accusations and the toll they took on innocent lives, leaving us with a sense of the profound injustices that can occur when systems fail and those in power turn a blind eye.

In Chapter 2, we witnessed the persistence of injustice as victims fought for their rightful exoneration. Legal battles and setbacks served as formidable obstacles on their path to justice, but their resilience and determination never wavered. These stories reminded us that the pursuit of truth and fairness often requires unwavering dedication and unwavering support.

Chapter 3 introduced us to the heroic figure of Alan Bates and the group of sub-postmasters who launched legal action against the Post Office. Their collective strength and the alliances they forged showcased the power of solidarity in the face of adversity. It was a testament to the indomitable spirit of individuals who refused to be silenced or sidelined.

Then, we turned our attention to "Mr. Bates vs The Post Office," a game-changing television drama that captured the hearts of millions. This series not only provided an overview of the scandal but also resonated on a deeply emotional level. It reminded us that storytelling, when done right, has the power to evoke empathy, spark conversations, and drive meaningful change.

Chapter 5 illuminated the impact unleashed by the series, revealing the overwhelming public reaction and support it garnered. Paula Vennells' decision to return her honor, driven by a petition signed by millions, demonstrated the potency of public opinion. The government's promise of a new law to swiftly exonerate and compensate victims was a testament to the tangible outcomes that television could achieve.

In Chapter 6, we revisited historical instances of TV dramas driving change, drawing lessons from "Cathy Come Home" and "When They See Us." These examples reinforced the idea that television has a rich history of influencing public perception and policy. They showcased the enduring power of stories that resonate deeply with audiences.

Chapter 7 expanded our exploration to include other TV series that addressed pressing social issues, such as "It's a Sin," "Pose," and "Dopesick." These shows demonstrated how television could educate, challenge stereotypes, and advocate for marginalized communities. They left an indelible mark on both viewers and society at large.

In Chapter 8, we delved into TV's role in shaping public perception and its impact on policy and public discourse. We recognized that television's potential to raise awareness extended beyond individual viewers, mobilizing communities, advocacy groups, and policymakers. Television's unique ability to create shared experiences and drive collective action remained a potent force for change.

Lastly, in Chapter 9, we looked toward the future, exploring upcoming TV projects that continued to address social issues. These projects signaled television's enduring commitment to amplifying voices and stories that deserve recognition. They reflected the medium's ability to adapt to changing times and embrace new formats while staying true to its mission of storytelling.

In conclusion, television remains a vital force in our world—a storyteller with the power to change lives, perspectives, and societies. It's a medium that bridges gaps, raises voices, and fosters understanding. Through the lens of television, we've witnessed the resilience of the human spirit, the importance of empathy, and the transformative impact of storytelling. As we navigate an ever-evolving media landscape, let us remember that the legacy of television in addressing social issues is not just a chapter in history; it's an ongoing narrative that continues to shape our world. Television, as a conduit for stories that matter, reminds us that our collective journey toward a better, more compassionate society is far from over. It's a journey that television will continue to walk with us, illuminating the path forward.